Praise for
FACE IT & FIX IT

"Mac doesn't pull any punches with *Face It & Fix It*.
This is a wakeup call for every owner of a struggling business".

Kevin Green, Self-Made Multi-Millionaire &
Leading Wealth Creation Expert (www.kevingreen.co.uk)

"There is a proven way of turning around the fortunes
of a business and Mac teaches that process brilliantly in
his book *Face It & Fix It*".

Gerry Robert (Bestselling author of Publish A Book & Grow Rich).

"Every business struggles at some point. Some don't survive
at all, some come out of it and tick along while others go
on to achieve huge success. In *Face It & Fix It* Mac Attram
shows you how to be in that elusive third group".

Adam Markel, CEO, Attorney, Bestselling Author of Pivot:
The Art & Science of Reinventing Your Career and Life.

"If your business is in trouble and you don't know where to
turn for help, the answer is this book, *Face It & Fix It*".

Clinton Swaine (The World's Leading Trainer of Experiential Games).

"My message to the owner of any struggling business is to not wait another minute. Square up to reality and read *Face It & Fix It* ... Fast" !

Marcus de Maria (Internationally acclaimed wealth expert)
www.marcusdemaria.com

"Mac is the BEST in the world for what he is doing now. He has produced a very well-structured and comprehensive guide to SUCCESS in business. It is a real gem. I would recommend this book to anyone".

Richard & Veronica Tan (Success Resources –
The World's Number 1 Seminar Company www.SRPL.net)

"The advice that Mac offers in *Face It & Fix It* should be taught at every business school".

Andy Harrington (Author of Passion Into Profit www.passionintoprofit.co.uk)

"*Face It & Fix* It is the shot in the arm that every owner of a struggling business needs".

T. Harv Eker, author of the #1 NY Times and International bestselling book Secrets of the Millionaire Mind.

"*Face It & Fix* it is an absolute must-read if your business is in trouble or if you are ready to take your business to the next level" !

Bill Walsh America's Small Business Expert

FACE IT
& FIX IT

HOW TO AVOID DISASTER AND TURN AROUND YOUR SMALL BUSINESS

MAC ATTRAM

Dedication

*To my wife, Linda, and my three children
T'yanna-Nicole, Destiny and Brandon
for your ongoing support and understanding as
I continue to follow my life's mission.*

*Also to my parents, Frederick and Eva,
for imbuing me with my thirst for
knowledge and understanding.*

Acknowledgements

I'd like to thank the following people.

Steve Roche, my editor, for helping me to shape this book.

Blair Singer for giving me the belief that I could be a trainer & speaker and providing me with the techniques and ongoing support.

T. Harv Eker for helping me to discover and live my life mission and purpose. Michelle Burr for giving me a platform to deliver my message to the world.

Richard and Veronica Tan (Success Resources), for giving me a platform to speak to thousands of people globally each year.

The W5s for their ongoing support, encouragement and ideas.

My team at **MindSpace Associates** for their commitment and dedication to train, coach & support individuals and business owners in their pursuit of growth & more happiness.

Contents

Foreword

The number of people plunging into the world of business ownership is amazing. More than ever. But the number of those small businesses that fail is devastating. I am sure you know the numbers. 80-95% gone inside of three years. And with them go the dreams, visions and aspirations of thousands of hard working and well intended individuals. What was, in one moment, a vibrant spirited plan of contribution and wealth, becomes a painful, cynical blood stained memory of struggle. Why?

It certainly is not lack of passion or hard work in most cases. It is something however that they do not teach you in school. For any entrepreneur who has ever had a plan to conquer the world and didn't, what they failed to realize that minute they made the decision to be a business owner, the minute they strapped on the gear and ran out onto the playing field, the minute the whistle blew to start the game......the game changed.

At that point it no longer is a game of just business development. It is primarily a game of personal development. It becomes a game about developing your strength, your resiliency, your ability to handle adversity, the ability to get up after getting knocked down again and again. It's a game of very high highs that can be followed by very low lows. The business becomes a test of your will and your ability to grow personally.

In most cases, the problem is lack of knowledge. Business knowledge and personal development knowledge. But nothing is obvious to the uninformed. Most do not know that the lack of knowledge in these two areas is what has blown a hole in the side of their ship which is now sinking. Money dries up, resources disappear, and the pressure mounts. For the uniformed business owner, the causes of their demise unfortunately becomes about everything or everyone else.

But there is a lifeline. Even better, there is a better way to prepare for the game. A better way to build your ship. It's with the knowledge that was never taught in school. Knowledge that only could come from someone who has lived and mastered the storm.

Mac's book is your lifeline if you are in a small business now. It is your blueprint if you are considering starting your own business. He has uncovered every pitfall, obstacle and danger that you could possibly face and gives you simple steps to fix or avoid them. Most importantly, he will give you the personal development wakeup call to face the reality of what lies ahead or what is right in front of you. That's what every entrepreneur needs.

I have known and worked with Mac for many years. He is an amazing entrepreneur. And you can find successful entrepreneurs if you look for them, but a successful entrepreneur that can TEACH you how to be successful is a whole other talent that he has shared with thousands of folks like yourself across five continents over the last ten years.

As an accomplished and disciplined martial artist, father and husband of an amazingly beautiful family, he is one of the very few individuals in the world of coaching and training who has truly "earned the right" to coach you to your business dreams. You are in the hands of a man who is not only a great teacher, but has an amazing heart for you to win. Now go Face it, Fix it and get your Dreams!!

Blair Singer – Entrepreneur, bestselling author, Rich Dad Advisor to Robert Kiyosaki Author of: Sales Dogs, Team Code of Honour, Little Voice Mastery

PART 1:

FACE IT

In my decade and a half of working with small businesses I have often seen owners and managers not face up to reality. Refusing to accept that there is a difficult situation that must be dealt with never works.

I used to do the same myself. But after a while I came to realize that running away from my problems was a race that I never seemed to win. Somehow or other when I ran away from my problems, they seemed to catch up with me again. Perhaps not straightaway. But eventually, there they were again.

I had to face up to my problems in the end. And by the time I did, the problems had become bigger than before and, to make it worse, I was mentally tired from running away from them.

I learned the hard way that it is always best to face problems head on. They're always easier to overcome when you do that. If you face a problem when it first appears you are at your strongest and it is at its weakest. It isn't always easy doing this of course because a problem can seem scary even when it first appears. But problems don't go away and they're always scarier when they come back in the future.

An important point to make is that when we run away from a problem, it's not the problem itself which is the issue. It's the fact that it is scary. We wouldn't run away from a problem if we didn't fear it, would we? Why would we?

The problems we deal with are the ones that are not scary. We gain strength when we face our fears. Our head clears and we are ready for action. Overcoming the problem may still be difficult, but at least we have a better chance of fixing it. We are in the driving seat.

Running away is about fearing what might happen. In most cases it won't be anywhere near as bad as we fear. The key is to not allow fear to be in charge.

I made this mistake myself. When I ran my first business I had problems I didn't face up to. The first mistake I made is that I started the business for the wrong reasons.

Before I became an entrepreneur I worked as a retail manager for a computer company. It wasn't long before I caught the bug and wanted to start my own business. I decided that IT would be a good field to get into. I thought it had potential and that I could make a lot of money. But I didn't have enough technical expertise or a passion for it. Because I didn't have the necessary IT knowledge I had to hire people that did. That was a cost to the business that I hadn't foreseen.

It became a struggle. I was working long hours, putting in up to 80 hours a week. I did that nonstop for almost 2 years and I suffered with burnout eventually. I was unhappy and that was an additional drain on my energy. I embarked on studying what really works in business by reading books and attending seminars. I fixed and sold the business, not for as much as I would have liked, but now it was no longer a burden on me. The signs were there early on but I refused to face up to them.

Things changed for me as an entrepreneur when I realized where I had been going wrong. I resolved at that point to face up to and not ignore problems in the future.

"People who succeed have momentum.
The more they succeed, the more they
want to succeed, and the more they find a
way to succeed. Similarly, when someone
is failing, the tendency is to get on a
downward spiral that can even become
a self-fulfilling prophecy."

Tony Robbins

So how is your small business doing? Be honest. No business is without its difficulties but some problems can have more catastrophic consequences for a business than others.

The Reasons Why Businesses Fail

In any walk of life, *knowing what not to do* can be as important as knowing what to do. This is particularly true in business. Neither school nor being an employee prepares us for being a business owner. Mistakes can be fatal.

There are many reasons why businesses fail. I have carried out extensive research and identified 43 problems that, if not dealt with, will lead to business failure.

First of all, let's define the issue. A business failure is when a company stops trading because it does not make a profit or does not bring in enough income to cover its expenses. Bear in mind that a profitable business can still fail – this happens if it does not generate enough cash flow to meet its expenses.

NOTE: The reasons for failure are deliberately not categorised or set out in any order of importance. This is because in my experience most owners of struggling small businesses have either:

- *avoided deeply thinking about the problems in their business; or thought shallowly about their problems and so have preconceived ideas about the areas in their business where their problems might exist.*

- *So in order to keep you on your toes as you read this chapter, the reasons for failure are set out in a random order.*

1. Leadership failure
The problem: Businesses do not just run themselves.

This is a major reason why businesses fail. Common leadership failings are:

- a lack of direction;
- someone not taking charge;
- problems being avoided;
- decisions not being made;
- a lack of vision, which results in a business drifting;
- insufficient experience at making strategic decisions; and
- not managing staff effectively.

Leadership is like captaining a ship. Irrespective of the size of a ship, it needs someone to be in charge. Without a captain it will sink, hit the rocks or arrive at the wrong destination.

A destination needs to be set for the ship and it needs to be steered throughout the journey. The crew (the staff) need to be managed and the passengers (the customers) need to be looked after. During the journey the ship may hit choppy waters or get diverted. So leadership is required by the captain so that the ship eventually arrives at its intended destination.

Leadership becomes a team effort as a business gets larger. Failings when a business is at this stage include disagreements within the leadership team on future direction and differences of opinion on how the business should be run.

Do you have any questions or pressing challenges at the moment? Book your FREE 30 Minute Business Success Session (value of $497) now at www.faceitandfixitbook.com

---

"Leadership is the capacity to
translate vision into reality."

Warren Bennis

2. Lacking uniqueness and value
The problem: Failing to offer real value and stand out in the crowd.

No matter the industry there is huge competition around these days. So many businesses fail because they do not differentiate themselves sufficiently from the companies they compete with.

History shows that having a great product or service for which there is a strong demand is not always enough. This is often because the approach taken towards marketing and sales is mediocre. When there is strong demand for a product or service there are normally a lot of competitors. To win in this environment businesses need to find a way of standing out in the crowd.

3. Failing to understand customer needs
The problem: Being out of touch with the marketplace.

Businesses can get complacent. Customers liking what you offer is not always enough these days. People are becoming more demanding. Businesses run into trouble when, on an ongoing basis, they do not seek feedback from their current customers and do not tune into what prospective customers want.

"It is better to fail in originality
than to succeed in imitation."

Herman Melville

"A man must be big enough to admit his mistakes, smart enough to profit from them, and strong enough to correct them."

John C. Maxwell

4. A poor business model
The problem: Having an inadequate plan for how to make money.

Businesses do not succeed if they don't know where they fit within the market. They fail when they are not clear on the precise value they offer and, from that, don't work out what they can get paid for and by whom. Too many businesses run into trouble because they operate without proven revenue streams.

5. Poor financial management
The problem: Not dealing with money properly.

Money does not look after itself. It needs to be managed. Failing to manage money is a common reason why businesses fail.

Financial management is the efficient and effective management of money. The aim is to manage it in such a way as to accomplish the objectives of the business. Financial management involves planning, directing, monitoring, organizing, and controlling money.

Only 40% of small businesses show a profit. 30% breakeven and 30% make a loss. Often financial performance can be improved by getting a grip on what is going on. Knowing the numbers in terms of money coming in and the money going out is crucial.

Too often people start a business with a dream of making money but don't have the inclination to learn how to manage their cash flow, to sort out their taxes or to control their expenses.

In fact, some business owners are useless with anything to do with money. You cannot be that way. Poor management of money and inadequate accounting practices put a business directly on the path to failure.

Many a business failure could have been avoided if a contingency fund were built up when times were good in order to weather things out when times were not so good.

"You make mistakes.
Mistakes don't make you."

Maxwell Maltz

6. Growing too quickly
The problem: Rapid growth which the business cannot deal with.

Fast growth is often what business owners think they want. But businesses who grow too fast often run into a unique set of problems and they can go under as a result. Examples of the problems include:

- not having the cash available to buy stock to fulfil their orders;
- investing too heavily into expansion; and
- having stock that cannot be sold.

7. Wrong motives
The problem: Starting in business for the wrong reasons

Businesses can fail because the business owner becomes disenchanted. Reasons provide motivation and motivation is a source of energy. So it's crucial to start a business for empowering reasons.

Sometimes people start a business to escape from a job they hate. The sole reason some people start their own business is that they want to make a lot of money. Some think that having their own business will allow them to spend more time with their family. Some are attracted to the idea that being their own boss means not having to answer to anyone else.

It's OK to want these things but you should always start a business with your eyes open. Sometimes entrepreneurs end up disappointed because they don't get the benefits they were seeking.

"Stop chasing the money and
start chasing the passion."

Tony Hsieh, CEO of Zappos

8. Poor business management
The problem: Failing to deal with or control the processes and people

Just as businesses fail because they fail to adequately manage money, they also fail because they don't properly manage their people or the operations of the business.

The management role is to coordinate the efforts of people to accomplish the goals of the business by using resources efficiently and effectively. This includes planning, organizing, staffing, directing and controlling.

It is common for entrepreneurs to not have the kind of management skills that running a business needs. Expertise in areas such as finance, purchasing, selling, production, and hiring and managing employees can be required. It is important to know what you can and can't do and to get help in areas where you are weak.

You've got to know what you do and don't do well from a management point of view and seek help when needed.

Successful managers also create a work climate that encourages productivity. Good managers need to be skilled at hiring competent people, training them and being able to delegate.

9. Inability to take a business to the next level
The problem: Having the skills to start a business, but not to grow it.

Some companies stall and then fail once they have established themselves. Companies that are successful early on possess the management skills needed at the beginning but, as the business grows, they don't have the different management skills which are then required.

To take a business to the next level once it has survived the difficult early years requires a different set of skills. This includes charisma, boldness, vision, creativity, networking skills, courage and attention to detail.

10. Insufficient capital
The problem: Not having enough operating funds.

Even though they have the potential to be successful, it's not uncommon for a business to fail because it doesn't have enough cash to stay in business long enough to get to the point where it can be successful.

Having insufficient operating funds is a fatal mistake. Business owners often underestimate how much money is needed and are forced to close before they have had a fair stab at achieving success.

11. Vague thinking
The problem: Failing to coherently and intelligently think through important aspects of the business.

Vague thinking in business never cuts it. Clarity is power. Many a business has failed because of woolly thinking. It is necessary to be precise and clear about issues such as points of differentiation, the market and buying habits.

The most important area when it comes to the need for clarity is the answer to this question – who are your customers? Too many businesses when asked this very basic question are not able to clearly state in one or two sentences who their customers are.

"The number one reason most people
don't get what they want is that they
don't know what they want."

T. Harv Eker

12. Location
The problem: Being in the wrong place can be an issue even for the best-run businesses.

Location is critical to the success of almost every business. A good business location may enable a struggling business to survive and thrive, but a bad location can spell disaster for even the best-managed enterprise.

Factors when it comes to location include being close to customers and issues like traffic, accessibility and parking.

These days location on the Internet and social media presence can be just as important as physical presence.

13. Inadequate or poor planning
The problem: Failing to think ahead.

Many a business has failed by just thinking about the here and now. Writing a business plan forces you to think in a thorough way and to think about problems that might hit in the future.

You must have a business plan. Writing a plan is like thinking in writing instead of in your head. The process of writing a business plan forces you to crystallise your thoughts.

A business plan doesn't have to be a huge document. But the process of researching and writing a business plan forces you to think through all aspects of your business. It helps prepare you to handle problems when they may arise in the future. A business plan helps you to define and focus on your goals and on your mission.

Anyone who has ever been in charge of a successful major event knows that were it not for their careful, methodical, strategic planning – and hard work – success would not have followed. The same could be said of most business successes.

"Failing to plan is
planning to fail."

Alan Lakein

14. Having no exit strategy

The problem: The owner or owners not planning for how they will eventually leave the business, and it going under due to a sense of drift.

As a captain of a ship, you wouldn't get your vessel to its intended destination and stay on board without disembarking, would you? 60% of business owners want to leave their business within ten years but have no idea how they'll do it. Owners run the risk of leaving things to chance and the business floundering as a result by not having thought this issue through.

15. Unrealistic expectations

The problem: Planning on being profitable too early on.

It is not realistic to expect massive success from day one but many new business owners make this mistake. It normally takes at least a year to build a profitable business. Many aspiring business owners think that most businesses succeed and are lucrative from the get-go. This is usually not the case. Depending on the type of business you have there is a way of being profitable from day one.

But generally speaking, it usually takes at least a year to develop a profitable business. The first year's goal is usually to break even. Even if a profit is made in the first year that money should normally be reinvested back into the business. In other words, in your first year, you should have other sources of income to live on.

"Planning is bringing the future into the present so that you can do something about it now."

Alan Lakein

16. An inability to commit
The problem: Failing to dedicate fully to the business

Even though most people would like to start their own business, only a small percentage actually make the leap. In order for a business idea to become a reality, a willingness is required to do due diligence on that idea, weigh up the facts and then make a prompt decision as to whether to start or not. When push comes to shove, most would-be entrepreneurs lack the self-confidence to make a decision and to act on it.

So even though it takes a lot of courage to even start a business, many small business owners go under because they start but approach running it in a hesitant and half-hearted way. So you owe it to yourself that, if you do make the leap, you at least give it your all.

17. An unwillingness to take responsibility
The problem: Getting into the blame game can lead to disaster.

A business owner is 100% responsible for his or her mistakes. Any time you start a business, there's always a risk of an outright business failure or a less-than-expected financial return. If that happens, the business owner cannot blame that on anyone else.

Responsibility has to be taken, no matter how difficult that might be to do. The business owner has to be prepared to be accountable. If things go wrong, no other person nor any external circumstance can be blamed.

"You need to make a commitment, and once you make it, then life will give you some answers."

Les Brown

18. Failing to communicate marketing messages which are clear, concise and compelling

Many business owners come up with a good point of differentiation but then fail to get that very message out in an effective way.

19. A stale marketing message
The problem: Failing to refresh the promotional messages.

Big companies sometimes tweak or completely revamp their marketing but smaller businesses often neglect to do this. Research by the National Small Business Association in the US found that over half of small businesses have no plans to try out new marketing ideas. That's a very perilous situation for a business to be in, unless its current marketing is working exceptionally well.

Big companies know that it's vital to refresh their branding and their promotional activities every so often. A perfect example of this is what the car rental company Avis did a few years ago. In 2012 they abandoned their 50-year-old strapline of "We try harder" and replaced it with "It's your space". Their old message had become stale so the comfort of the interiors of their cars is now what sets them apart.

20. Overconfidence
The problem: Assurance is a great quality to have but can be a weakness if the business idea is a bad one or if the execution is poor.

Many a business has hit the rocks because of the bullishness of the founder, which is why market research and testing are so important.

It's not always the case obviously, but sometimes critics of a new business concept are right. Some business ideas are ill-conceived. Sometimes business ideas are solid but are ill-timed. Founders should support their gut instinct by testing out their ideas and carrying out market research.

"I think we tried very hard not to be overconfident, because when you get overconfident, that's when something snaps up and bites you."

Neil Armstrong

21. A poor pricing strategy
The problem: Mistaken approaches to pricing which lead to loss-making.

Pricing errors are all too common and can be a killer for any business. Some of the most common pricing mistakes are as follows.

- Basing prices on solely on costs and not taking perceptions of value into account.
- Pricing in line with the rest of the market, which leads to the commoditization of your product or service.
- Holding prices at the same level for too long as this makes it very difficult to ever increase prices.
- Changing prices without anticipating the possible reaction of competitors.

22. Failure to adequately anticipate cash flow
The problem: Failing to operate by the old adage of 'cash is king'.

This is the single biggest reason why businesses fail. You need to account for the fact that suppliers will want to be paid quickly. Any business selling on credit needs to plan for the fact that they might not get paid for many weeks or months. When you are just starting out, suppliers want quick payment.

This call on cash from two sides can pull a business down if they fail to plan for it.

23. Conflict

The problem: Hostile arguments can destroy trust and morale and can eventually destroy a business.

Unfortunately disputes are all too common in small businesses. While there is nothing wrong with spirited debate, constant wrangles can drain the life out of a business.

Most start-up teams fail to plan for the possibility that a partner may want to leave at some point. Never assume a business partner will be in it for the long haul. Circumstances can change and this can lead to conflicts.

To exacerbate the problem, written shareholder agreements are often not created and signed.

I regret not having a written shareholders' agreement in my first business. One of my fellow shareholders just disappeared one day leaving us in debt. The other one was responsible for sales and marketing but wasn't very effective. So I ended up working very long hours and suffered from burnout.

"You don't understand burnout unless you've been burned out. And it's something you can't even explain. It's just doing something you have absolutely no passion for."

Elena Delle Donne

24. Burnout

The problem: Initial energy and excitement can eventually dissipate.

This can happen for many reasons but, when it does, it can quickly bring a business to its knees. Most businesses feed off the owner's energy and excitement. When that eagerness to succeed is missing the business can quickly die.

What can happen is that over time the owner gets tired as they get older or has a change of priorities. Sometimes they lose their drive or become sick of the business.

Owning a business requires a huge investment of time, money, energy and emotion. In the early days it's easy to work long days and forget to take time off. But in the end, this can cause burnout. When this happens motivation and creativity can suffer. A negative and pessimistic attitude can develop and prevail. It's not unusual for business owners to find themselves unable to balance their business and personal lives. In the end, both worsen.

25. Failure to join the online world

The problem: A surprisingly large number of small businesses still aren't making the most of the opportunities which digital technologies offer to win new customers and to service existing ones better.

Most people these days spend many hours of the day staring at the screens of their computers, tablets and smart-phones. A large percentage of small businesses are missing out on this opportunity and are suffering as a consequence.

A survey conducted in the USA by the National Small Businesses Association found that, while 82% of businesses have a website, 72% of firms do not sell their products or services online. And few small firms are making the most of opportunities to dive into the mobile market which is a great way to reach younger consumers. Only 18% have a mobile website, the survey found.

Simply put, every business should have a website. At the very least, every business should have a professional looking and well-designed site that enables users to easily find out about their business and how to avail themselves of their products and services. Businesses that don't are most likely losing business to those that do.

26. Cyber theft

The problem: Data breaches can be the death knell to a small business.

Research shows that small businesses as well as the big well-known names are now being targeted by cyber criminals. 94% of small-business owners report being very or somewhat concerned about cyber-security and so they should.

60% of small businesses fail after a cyber-attack which is an astonishing statistic. Nearly half of small businesses report that they have been victims of a cyber-attack. For those whose bank accounts was hacked, the average loss was almost $7,000.

Despite the risks, most business owners don't turn to IT security professionals for help and this is a huge mistake.

27. Underestimating the competition

The problem: Owner Syndrome which is where a business falls into the trap of thinking that their product or service is better than the competition has to offer no matter what the evidence is to the contrary.

A fatal mistake is to undervalue a competitor no matter what their size, what stage they are at or where they are.

Even if you are a David in a world of Goliaths, it doesn't mean the Goliaths will be the only threat to your continued existence. You need to be just as wary of new players in your industry. Unfortunately, business owners often underestimate the new kid on the block.

Sometimes it may not be a competitor's superior product that can put a company out of business. The competitor may win out on a factor such as speed or convenience. Customers are not always loyal and they will go to where they feel they're getting the best overall offering.

28. Procrastination and poor time management

The problem: Being badly organised and putting off jobs can be disastrous.

Continually putting off tasks that you don't enjoy doing will sink your business faster than anything else. You can't afford to waste time on unimportant tasks while critical jobs pile up.

All tasks need to be done. If you don't want to do an important job or don't want to spend the time doing them, you must hire someone else to carry them out for you.

If your time management and prioritizing skills are poor then learn or hire someone that can help.

"Procrastination is like a credit card:
it's a lot of fun until you get the bill."

Christopher Parker

29. Overreliance on one customer
The problem: When one customer becomes the source of 30% or more of a small company's total revenue.

One of the goals of most small companies is to develop a number of large, steady customers. This is the foundation for long-term growth and stability. Having customers you can count on month after month with secure cash flow gives an entrepreneur the opportunity to consider expanding.

But when one customer accounts for almost a third of all revenues then your company is in the danger zone. Very real and even potentially catastrophic financial dangers can emerge. That customer could suddenly cancel all orders or cut back sharply, and then cash flow would be badly disrupted. It happens and has taken many a small business out over the years.

30. Overreliance on one product or service

Similarly being too dependent on one offering can leave a business vulnerable.

31. Disgruntled employees
The problem: Unhappy staff can hurt profitability and lose customers for a business.

This is a large scale issue. A survey of American workers conducted in 2013 by Gallup found that 7 out of 10 are not engaged at work.

Unhappy staff don't perform at a high level. They don't put in an extra effort or work late when needed. These are the kind of efforts that small businesses with potential need if they are to make it.

32. Mistakenly thinking that a hobby can be turned into business

Just because you love something don't automatically assume that it can be a money-maker. It might be but it is wrong to assume it can.

33. Overexcitement about new ideas

Through their very nature, entrepreneurs often get excited about new ideas. The problem they sometimes have is evaluating whether an idea is a real opportunity or not and, if it is, properly implementing it.

34. Poor record keeping and financial controls

As boring as it may be, you must maintain accurate business data, file tax returns on time and stay on top of the financials.

35. Lack of industry experience

Although entering a market with fresh thinking and new ideas can be an advantage, you must at least understand your industry as it is now, know the trends and be aware of the skills and knowledge required to be part of it.

If you don't know about these things and don't have the basic skills, you should educate yourself. Talk to others who are successfully running their own businesses, talk to industry leaders, get a book, find a website, do your homework. And don't stop there – keep increasing your business and industry skills by continually attending seminars and workshops and reading new books.

36. Ineffective sales approaches

The problem: Not leading potential customers down the road to a sale.

Lack of sales is a widespread issue. But the shame is that the small businesses who fail due to lack of sales could have likely avoided disaster by tweaking their approach in a few simple ways.

Research shows that 8% of sales people generate 80% of the sales. Perseverance is the common missing ingredient. Too many poorly performing sales people give up after just one or two knockbacks.

People in business often hope and expect to do business the first time they meet a prospect. Yet studies reveal that only 2% of sales occur when two parties meet for the first time. It's extraordinary how often potential customers express an interest in a product or service, but never hear back again.

Only 20% of sales leads are ever followed up. In other words, 8 out of 10 potential opportunities are lost without trace simply due to lack of follow-up.

37. Poor customer service

The problem: Failing to look after customers once they've bought.

Too often small businesses having worked hard to gain a customer, throw it all away. It is important to attend to all the other things which matter to customers such as returning phone calls and replying to emails promptly, invoicing correctly and being pleasant and professional in all face-to-face dealings.

Word soon gets around and poor service, if it continues on a long-term basis, will bring a business down.

38. Inflexibility

The problem: Not being open to new ideas and being afraid to experiment.

It is not uncommon for small business owners to become complacent. Market needs change. Failure can result from not monitoring trends and adjusting strategy when the marketplace is moving.

High profile examples of the danger of intransigence are what the Internet did to the music industry and the collapse of Blockbuster. Do you remember Blockbuster? Nothing stays the same forever.

Small businesses fail when they assume that what they have always done will always work. They are in dangerous territory if they don't challenge how they do things and don't look to adjust when new technologies and approaches become available.

39. Overgeneralization

It is a mistake to spread yourself too thinly and thereby reduce quality. Setting out to be everything to everyone is normally a guaranteed way of heading towards disaster. The market pays excellent rewards for excellent results, average rewards for average results, and below average rewards for below average results.

40. Thinking that you can do everything yourself
The problem: A business owner who finds it difficult letting go and giving up control.

Businesses get themselves into hot water when the boss has the attitude that he or she must always have hands-on control of every aspect of the business. The belief that they are the only person capable of making decisions is a dangerous one to have. No one person can do everything and make every decision. Nor should they try to.

The job of the boss should be to concentrate on what matters the most for the business and to get others to help out.

41. Not working hard enough

When managers and staff are not ready and willing to work hard, things can go wrong very quickly. It's as simple as that.

42. Ignoring legal issues

There is a tendency for business owners to think that lawyers are an expensive luxury. But unresolved legal problems have a habit of coming back to bite at the most inconvenient time. A competent lawyer can be worth their weight in gold.

"The price of success is hard work, dedication to the job at hand, and the determination that whether we win or lose, we have applied the best of ourselves to the task at hand."

Vince Lombardi

43. Poor administration

It may be boring, but ignoring the paperwork is always costly. Many business owners fail to devote proper time to administrative work. They find it boring. This unglamorous work must be done though.

In summary, the four main causes of business failure are:

- personal behaviour
- internal processes
- external factors
- financial challenges

Do you have any questions or pressing challenges at the moment? Book your FREE 30 Minute Business Success Session (value of $497) now at www.faceitandfixitbook.com

PART 2:

FIX IT

Any business can be saved, no matter how bad the situation may seem. Later on I am going to introduce you to the formula I used myself to save my own business and which I have used with my clients as a Business Coach and Turnaround Consultant.

But before I show you my process, it's worth examining how other companies have been turned around. As you read these inspiring stories, notice which of the 43 mistakes from the previous chapter these companies were making.

"Success is not final; failure is not fatal:
It is the courage to continue that counts."

Winston S. Churchill

SpotCo gets unstuck from a tricky spot

What you so often see with businesses that have been around for a while is that they get stuck. They start out and develop a way of working which works for a while. Then they find that they are working hard in the same way they always have, but are no longer making any progress.

Often they don't realise that they are stuck. Then they do, but don't know what to do about it. So they just keep working away in the way they always have in the hope that things will just turn around. Finally things get so bad that they realise they need to do something serious to sort things out. That's what happened at SpotCo.

The New York ad agency survived for nine years with a reactive and random approach to management. That way worked when they had just a few employees. But they were doing highly creative print and broadcast advertising projects for high-profile Broadway productions like *Rent* and *The History Boys* along with the ESPN and MTV TV networks. There was a lack of structure and leadership in some areas. The business was a disaster waiting to happen.

The company had grown to 40 employees but was organised in such a way that all decisions had to be made by the boss, Drew Hodges. Some staff had performance reviews and some didn't. There were arguments between the creative side of the business and the sales staff.

Things turned around when Hodges brought in the leadership expert and co-author of the book *Leadership on the Line*, Marty Linsky, to help him. The outcome was the implementation of a management structure that was able to support growth.

Linsky quickly realised that Hodges needed to break out of the rut he had got into and needed to develop leadership skills. He taught Hodges – a creative type with a strong personality – to listen more and to talk less. Linsky got Hodges to encourage his people to make their opinions known.

The end result was that the company began to work together for the common goals they had set for themselves. What they used to have was a creative genius running the show. But what they ended up with was many leaders. The company used to be run by a boss who was part-parent and part-peacemaker. The eventual outcome was that routine issues were solved by the workforce and not by the boss. Senior managers began to focus on dealing with the strategic and not the day-to-day issues.

SeeMore does more

It is no good having a good product if no one knows about it. It is also tough to make it big if all you have is one product, no matter how good it is. This is a story about a company that made these mistakes for seven years.

Payne Stewart won the U.S. Open in 1999 using a little-known putter from a virtually unknown company called the SeeMore Putter Company. Being in the international spotlight in that way could have been the making of the company, but it didn't work out that way for SeeMore and it struggled.

Fortunately, one man had never gotten SeeMore out of his mind. His name was Jim Grundberg and he got together with Jason Pouliot to buy the company. They had both previously worked at the rival company, Odyssey.

The year was 2006 and they set about attempting to turn the fortunes of SeeMore around. Within three years sales had grown from $50,000 to $1.5 million. Their approach was simple – they focused on developing new products and marketing.

In 2006 SeeMore was selling just one product, an innovative putter with a uniquely designed head. So the duo quickly set about bringing out new products. They knew the golf business having worked in it themselves, but they also carried out research with professional players and other key people in the industry. From this, they embarked on an ambitious plan to create and market a new range of premium putters.

Their approach to marketing included being present at professional events. They would showcase their range of putters during practice days in the hope that pro players and their caddies would stop to take a look. They weren't trying to sell but gave their products away in the hope that the players would try them out.

SeeMore also began to highlight famous players in its marketing who use their products. Zach Johnson, for example, won the 2007 Masters and The Open in 2015 using a SeeMore putter and the company used those major achievements to its advantage.

What Jim and Jason did was to take a good thing and to make it better. It developed momentum. They took a single, high quality product and built on it. They widened the range whilst remaining in their product niche, namely putters. And they physically got themselves out into the marketplace and mixed with the people that they knew would lend credibility to their offerings, namely professional players.

Sparton's gladiator saves the century-old manufacturer

This is a story of survival for a small manufacturer but decline for the town where the company was born. The turnaround expert brought in to save Sparton, Cary Wood, decided to cut ties after 109 years with the troubled company's headquarters in Jackson, Michigan. It got very ugly but that brave act turned out to be a turning point for Sparton itself.

The defence and medical manufacturing company had been in trouble for quite some time. In 2008, for example, it lost $13 million. At one point they were told by the bank that, unless something radical happened in the following 2 months, the company would be bankrupt.

The turnaround that followed was dramatic, though. Sales increased by more than 20% in the four years from 2009 to 2013. Sparton acquired 8 companies and doubled revenues.

Where the management team that preceded Cary Wood went wrong was to grow in a relentless way. In the process they took on customers too quickly, failed to operate the manufacturing side of things effectively and ended up losing money on every dollar they brought in. They also failed to communicate effectively with their shareholders.

Cary Wood's first actions when he arrived were to temporarily stop company payments to the pension and 401(k) schemes. He began laying off employees, dropping unprofitable customers and renegotiating contracts. He personally monitored the money going in and the money going out of the company's bank accounts from dawn until dusk. If a customer was late in paying an invoice, an employee was physically dispatched to go and chase payment.

Shutting down the company's presence in its birthplace in Jackson was obviously hugely controversial. During the difficult period Cary Wood told his team to not visit local restaurants and to generally lay low. He also swapped his expensive Mercedes for a Jeep.

This story has two sides to it, though. All that remains of the Sparton plant in Jackson now is rubble because an arson attack burnt it to the ground. Sparton has grown to now employing 1,500 people and has replaced high-volume/low-margin manufacturing work with precision products in lower volume.

Apple goes from irrelevance to iconic status

When you look at where Apple is now, it is easy to forget where the company was in the mid-1990s. It had lost ground massively to Microsoft and was a very minor player in the IT marketplace. No less a figure than Michael Dell back in 1995 had said that he would have closed the company down if he were running it.

Steve Jobs thought differently though when he returned in 1997 to take the reins again of the company he founded. In fact, "Think Different" was the title of an advertising campaign that Apple ran soon after he returned.

That phrase encapsulates what Steve Jobs did to turn around the fortunes of the iconic tech company. How did he do it? He did indeed think differently, he innovated and he wasn't afraid to be controversial.

The turnaround he engineered is nothing short of outstanding. In his time there, the stock price increased by over 8,500% and revenues increased by over 820%. Here are six ways that Steve jobs went about his job.

1. He hated mundane products. Jobs made sure that Apple's products were not only innovative in and of themselves, but he also ensured that they were integrated. So iPods, iPads, iTunes, iPhones and the App Store were all engineered to work together.

2. He knew that customers don't always know what they want. Apple doesn't run focus groups. It has a track record of intuitively creating new products and then persuading customers to buy those products that they wouldn't previously have thought that they wanted.

3. Jobs wasn't afraid to go back to basics and change what the company was all about. It began as a computer company but Jobs broadened out Apple's product offerings. To symbolise this transformation, the company's name was changed in 2007 from Apple Computer, Inc. to Apple Inc.

4. He wasn't afraid to break with convention. Traditionally tech companies have not been retailers. But Steve Jobs wasn't happy with the way in which stores were positioning and merchandising Apple's products. So Jobs decided to get into retail and create Apple Stores. Needless to say, he decided to do retail differently and the shops have become hugely successful and have shaken up the way in which retail is done.

5. Jobs knew the huge importance of aesthetics. Computer products historically had never looked good. Function had always come before form. Apple changed that by making their products look beautiful. Jobs knew that if he could make them desirable objects then they would fly off the shelves. It started with iMacs being colourful and has continued with the sleekness and desirability of the way in which iPods, iPhones and iPads look and feel.

6. Jobs was never afraid to try anything. Apple and Microsoft were sworn enemies just like Coca-Cola and Pepsi. But when Jobs took over the company again in 1997 it had been losing money for 12 years. So what did Steve Jobs do? He approached Bill Gates and what followed was a $150 million investment into Apple. That enabled Apple to finally achieve financial stability. Both companies ended up winners when they previously had been fierce competitors.

Do you have any questions or pressing challenges at the moment? Book your FREE 30 Minute Business Success Session (value of $497) now at www.faceitandfixitbook.com

"Be a yardstick of quality.
Some people aren't used to
an environment where
excellence is expected."

Steve Jobs, ex-Chairman & CEO of Apple

IBM reinvents itself

Louis V. Gerstner was a complete outsider to IBM when he arrived with the job of turning around what was then an 82-year-old company. Gerstner recounts that he needed to be that in order to save the computing giant. For example, coming in he had no emotional attachment to longsuffering IBM products like OS/2 software, whereas an insider might have had some kind of misplaced loyalty.

Gerstner had been the leader at RJR Nabisco and he took over as chairman and CEO of IBM on 1 April 1993. The situation he took over was no joke, however. But the turnaround he engineered was remarkable as, from 1993 to Gerstner's retirement in 2002, IBM's market capitalization rose from $29 billion to $168 billion.

The first thing Gerstner did at 'Big Blue' was to cut billions of dollars in costs in order to avoid bankruptcy. He slashed jobs and sold assets because the company was dangerously close to running out of cash.

He stopped the already-underway plan to break up the company into different units. He wanted to keep everything in place so that IBM could deliver complete technology solutions to its clients using its wide range of hardware, software and services. He thought that the company was too internally-focused and not sufficiently customer-focused. The different divisions were not working together. So one of Gerstner's major achievements during the turnaround was to change that ingrained corporate culture.

Gerstner set about doing this by relating each employee's pay to the performance of the whole company rather than to the division they worked at. He wanted staff to cooperate with other divisions.

The company changed so that teamwork and getting things done quickly were rewarded. Based on his maxim of people doing what you inspect rather than what you expect, he changed the way in which results were measured. Staff were asked to make personal commitments that helped IBM to achieve its corporate commitments. Salary was tied to how employees performed against these personal commitments.

Another way in which Gerstner brought about the unification of the company was to use just one advertising agency, namely Ogilvy & Mather. He wanted there to be one core marketing message for the whole company on a global basis.

By 2012, IBM had gone from near-bankruptcy to being ranked by *Fortune* magazine as the second largest U.S. firm in terms of number of employees, the fourth largest in terms of market capitalization and the ninth most profitable company.

"What I'm trying to do is deliver results, not promises; results, not vision; results, not concepts. The world is cynical about IBM's promises."

Louis V. Gerstner, Jr.

Props N Frocks Gets Fixed

www.propsnfrocks.co.uk

When Adele Wiseman and her mum started their business in 1998 the plan wasn't to create what they eventually did, namely the largest fancy dress shop in the county of Essex in the UK. The motivation back then was to provide better quality costumes to amateur dramatic groups.

When they opened they only stocked 4 costumes but the business grew over the next decade to having over 6,000 available for purchase and hire.

In the early days they supplied costumes based on what their customers were asking for. They kept standards high and grew mainly through word of mouth and leaflet drops. In time, they extended into other areas such as party wear and took on staff to cover the fact the large shop was open 7 days a week. Staff were also needed to maintain the for-hire costumes.

The shop is located a couple of miles away from the nearest village so there is no passing trade. The advantage of that, though, is that they attract very few time wasters because, if someone has taken the trouble to drive out to the shop, they are very likely to be looking to make a purchase.

It was always an uphill battle, but it was ten years on from starting out in 1998 when the problems began to come to a head. Fancy dress was dying and competition from the Internet was having an effect. Their overheads were high because of all the staff they needed to run the shop.

They had ideas on how to fix their business but it was an unexpected turn of events which lead to the eventual turnaround.

By this time, the business was very much a family affair with Adele's son and daughter now working alongside her and her mum. They were approached by a researcher about featuring in a forthcoming television programme about family businesses.

That never came to fruition but another TV project did. Their business was in trouble so they were asked if they wanted to take part in a new BBC-TV series called *The Fixer* featuring the well-known business trouble-shooter, Alex Polizzi. Because it was a BBC series, they felt confident it would be a quality production. A team of business analysts came in beforehand with lots of questions and filming took place over a 6-week period in autumn 2011.

Alex Polizzi's suggestions were not altogether surprising and Adele and family decided to run with them. They reduced their stockholding and shifted their business model more towards costume hire and away from costume sales. They took down the 'Do Not Touch' signs thus allowing customers to pick up and look at costumes they were considering hiring. They were able to bring money in by selling off some of their stock.

One of the problems is that people don't need to hire fancy dress costumes very often. So they decided to focus their costume hire efforts on particular times of the year such as Halloween and World Book Day. They also moved into new profitable areas such as mascots and themed children's parties.

Alex also encouraged Adele's son, Ellis, to play a more front of house role in the business. Previously he tended to hide himself away behind the scenes and not interact with customers. Ellis was pushed to the front and grew in confidence. He took on the mascot side of the business and began dealing with promotions companies.

They became creative and more targeted with their marketing. They gave mascots away for free to local schools who, in return, issued their flyers to the parents of the school children. They also became active on Facebook. The exposure the business received when the programme aired on BBC2 helped as well.

Adele and her family were open to the ideas and suggestions that Alex Polizzi made back in 2011. They openly admit that if they hadn't done so, then they would have been out of business within a year.

Chrysler engineers the greatest business turnaround of all time

Lee Iacocca is the man who turned around the fortunes of Chrysler. He joined just after being sacked by Ford in 1979 and took over at Chrysler as CEO and chairman not knowing a great deal about the company he was charged with saving.

His reign started at the point when Chrysler was announcing the worst loss in its history – $160 million in the third quarter of that year. Added to that, the energy crisis lead to the biggest recession to hit the USA in 50 years. Morale was low and Chrysler's range of vehicles were perceived as boring and poor quality. So it couldn't really have been worse. No-one could have guessed at what was to happen over the next 5 years, however.

Iacocca started by taking tens of thousands of cars out of production. He changed things around so that vehicles would no longer be built without orders from dealers. He also insisted that the dealerships held the inventory rather than Chrysler. He made major changes to the way the leasing side of the business worked.

On the people side of things, he replaced slackers with fast movers. He created a system of financial controls and quality control experts. He hired new marketing people who brought back the ram logo. An important step was to take some of the risk of buying a Chrysler away for customers. This was done by launching a money-back guarantee campaign including a zero-cost maintenance plan for two years.

Costs were cut by closing plants in Michigan and in Detroit. He introduced a just-in-time inventory arrangement with Chrysler's suppliers.

To raise money he sold real estate valued at $90 million and sold the Defence division to General Dynamics for $348 million. Massive layoffs of blue-collar and white-collar workers were made and this saved $500 million a year.

That was all very well but Iacocca still needed to do more because the financial situation was so bad. So he asked the federal government for loan guarantees. Up to $1.5 billion in loan guarantees were offered over the next year. All of Chrysler's assets were held as collateral by the government. When the loan guarantees were approved in 1979, Chrysler was $4.75 billion in debt. The banks had wanted Chrysler to declare bankruptcy. Chrysler still had to ask for another $400 million in loan guarantees in 1981.

But soon the turnaround started to kick in. Chrysler earned the best-ever profit figure of $925 million in 1983. Plants were modern and high-tech and half a million workers still had jobs. Exactly five years after he was fired from Ford the turnaround was complete when Iacocca presented a check for $813,487,500 to bankers in New York to pay back the loans.

"We are continually faced by great opportunities brilliantly disguised as insoluble problems."

Lee Iacocca, former President and CEO of Chrysler

The Fix It Formula

I am now going to set out the process I have developed for turning around the fortunes of any business. I used it myself in my own business and I have utilised it over the years with my clients in my work as a Business Coach & Consultant.

I call it The Fix It Formula and it is a systematic and comprehensive way of fixing the problems in every area and in every aspect of a business. You will notice that the first area that is fixed within the process is you as the leader of your business. Success starts and ends with the business leader.

No area of the business can be neglected, though, so make sure you work your way through the whole process and fix the problems you have within your business model, with marketing and branding, with sales, with financials, with culture, with operations, with staffing and with customer management. If you are experiencing growth problems, the last aspect of the Fix It Formula shows you how to resolve those issues.

1. How to Fix Leadership Problems

There are eight things you can do to instantly make you a better leader.

- Develop a vision and communicate it to your people. Paint a picture of it. Then ask your team what the vision is to ensure they are on the same page as you.

- Lead by example because leaders need to show and not just tell. If you want your employees to be punctual, make sure you're there on time – or even early. If professionalism is a priority, make sure you're dressed for success, and treat everyone you interact with (both in - person and online) with courtesy. Set the tone and your employees will follow it.

- Show humility because a leader shares the spotlight and is comfortable crediting others.

- Communicate effectively because great leaders make sure they are heard and understood but they also know the importance of listening. Communication is a two-way street.

- Keep meetings productive because time is money. Limit conversations going off on tangents and other time wasters during meetings.

- Find a mentor because the best leaders out there know when they need help, and they know where to turn to in order to get it.

- Be emotionally aware. Be sensitive to different points of view and different backgrounds. When using your head to do what's best for your company, don't forget to have a heart.

- Never stop learning and improving because great leaders are constantly learning and always trying to improve themselves. Be sure to keep your mind open to new ideas and possibilities.

- Adopt the right mindset. This is about mastering what my friend Blair Singer calls the Little Voice. Leaders have control over the voice that, if left in charge, feeds us with a stream of self-limiting and self-sabotaging thoughts.

"Effective leadership is not about
making speeches or being liked;
leadership is defined by results
not attributes."

Peter Drucker

2. How to Fix Business Model Problems

There is a lot of confusion and management-speak when it comes to the subject of business models. In simple terms, a business model is what you will do to make money. Answering the following questions will help you to define your own particular business model.

- Who are your target customers?
- What customer problem do you solve?
- What specific value do you deliver?
- How will you reach, acquire and retain your customers?
- How will you differentiate your offering?
- How will you generate revenue?
- What is your cost structure?
- What's your profit margin?

You need to figure out where the money will come from. Who will pay? How much? How often? What percentage of every sale will find its way to your bottom line as profit? What is the timeline for the money to start coming in? How will your customers pay? In other words, will they be paying in one lump sum or spreading the cost?

Examples of business models include developing a product and selling it directly to customers. Other models include selling wholesale to retailers, selling through distributors and licensing products to other companies.

> **Do you have any questions or pressing challenges at the moment? Book your FREE 30 Minute Business Success Session (value of $497) now at www.faceitandfixitbook.com**

3. How to Fix Marketing Problems

When thinking about marketing, it is important to start at the strategic level. Get very clear on your outcome and exactly what you want to achieve with your marketing efforts. Be clear on your goals, your objectives and the campaigns you will need to run in order to get to your desired destination.

Choose the best Marketing Methods

Your aim should be to set up marketing systems so that people constantly want to do business with you. Think of marketing as getting a horse to water. The job of sales is then to persuade the horse to drink the water.

Here are some approaches that you could take to get your horse to water.

- **Relationship Marketing** is where you strategically spend time building relationships with your prospective clients. The aim is, over a period of time, for them to get to know you, get to like you, and get to trust you. If they find that what you offer is of value, then they will continually want to do business with you.

- **Direct marketing** means that you go straight to the customer. So this could be in the form, for example, of a sales letter or a brochure that you mail to prospects using a mailing list. Your job as a direct marketer is to send your prospects relevant and compelling information.

- **Guerrilla marketing** is about approaching prospects in a very unconventional way.

- **Viral marketing** is about getting other people to share your material with their contacts on your behalf.

- **Word of mouth marketing** is when someone else is talking about your product and referring business to you.

- **Print advertising** can still work because a significant number of people still buy newspapers and magazines. It is a high risk form of marketing, however, as a typical response to a campaign is less than 1%.

- **TV and radio advertising** can be very expensive. So you need to very carefully select the stations you advertise on and the programmes you run your adverts in between.

- If you are a local business then **leaflets drops** are worth considering. You can expect a response rate of between 2% and 10%.

- **Incentives** in the form of discount cards and coupons can bring you new customers and retain existing ones.

- If your prospects need educating about what you do then it is worth considering doing **free talks.**

- There is an old saying that no publicity is bad publicity. This is one of the biggest aspects when it comes to **public relations** – knowing how to maximise the opportunities that good news represents and how to manage situations when things don't go right. Negative publicity can be turned into good publicity. But the problem is that some business owners are unaware on how to really use PR and also, they are unaware of some secrets about free PR. They think they have got to pay for large-scale advertorials. PR is a slow burner. Sometimes it takes a long time for your brand to get exposed. So, don't quit on PR too early.

- I write articles for a variety of publications and make myself available as an interviewee. Be aware of what is trending in the news and always be on standby.

- The other thing you can do is to write **blog posts,** either for your own website or as a guest blogger on someone else's website.

- **Awards** are a great way to get exposure and come with the added bonus of the built-in credibility that comes from winning or even being nominated for an award.

- Another way of marketing your business is to seek an **endorsement** from a celebrity. Lenovo benefited when they got Ashton Kutcher, an entrepreneur who invested in start-up tech companies, to endorse their computers. That created a lot of exposure for Lenovo.

"The aim of marketing is to know
and understand the customer so
well the product or service fits
him and sells itself."

Peter Drucker

4. How to Fix Branding Problems

Why is branding so important? If you get your branding right, you'll have people coming to you wanting to do business with you because they are already presold. They will do this based on what your brand says about you in terms of your reputation and your credibility.

People gravitate towards great brands. Your brand can create space in your prospect's mind. By space I mean you can grab their attention despite the fact we are all bombarded with so much information these days from media of all kinds. Your brand can say everything without saying anything.

Let's look at some examples. What does the Apple branding say to you? Innovative, creative, clean, user-friendly. Their customers are presold anytime Apple releases a new product.

When you think of the Domino's Pizza brand, what words and feelings come to mind? How about reliability because they deliver when they say they will deliver or you get your pizza for free. Their advertising is dynamic. It's blue and red and entices you to come and order from them. You know that they will always give you an offer or a special deal.

What does the Nike brand conjure up for you? It is about sports and high performance. It is about going the extra mile. It is about doing whatever it takes to get it out there, to get it done. Their slogan says it so well – *Just Do It.*

Step 1: Creating your branding

Start by thinking about your personal story and answer the following questions.

- How do customers **feel** when they interact with you?
- How do they **benefit** by using your product or service?
- What do they **get** by using your product or service?
- What **words** would people use to describe your services or products?
- What is **unique** about you?
- What is the **promise** that your customers get from you?
- What are the **standards** that you work to?
- What is the ultimate **message** of your business?

What sets your business apart from competitors? How do you conduct business in a way that is totally unique? What are your competitors doing better than you are? Develop a customized approach or service package that no one else in your industry is using so you can present it as a strong value proposition that attracts attention and interest.

This is how you start to build a brand. Your brand is the image your customers recognize and associate with your business. Your brand identity, including your logo, tagline, colours, and all the visible aesthetics and business philosophies that represent your company should be supported by your value proposition. It should separate you from the pack and present your individual perspective to your customers. Do everything you can to present that unique value proposition to your market so you can capture a market share and begin building your conversion rates.

To publicize your brand and set yourself apart, you will also need to step up your marketing plan and use as many avenues as possible to present your brand to the public. You may be far better than your competitors but that won't make any difference if your prospects don't even know you're in the game. Use social media, word of mouth, cold calling, direct mail, and other tried-and-trusted marketing techniques. Ensure you have a well-optimized online presence, develop lead generation and contact information capture techniques such as offering high-quality content on your site, a subscriber newsletter and information giveaways.

Step 2: Brand personality

Via your branding, are you communicating a confusing message to the marketplace in terms of who you are and what you do?

Consistency in your branding is crucial. Look at Apple. You can feel the brand, you can see the brand. It has a clear and definite personality.

So, the question here is what does your brand say about you? Does it convey and evoke words like trust or professionalism. Or is it fun? Is it exciting? Or is it more about reliability?

Why is it important to have a personality? The personality of your brand conveys a particular emotion or set of emotions. The personality is indicated by aspects such as the colours you use, the shape of your products and the packaging.

The leading brand in the world used to be Coca-Cola. Now it's Apple. Their colours are very clean. For example, they use black and white.

Black conveys boldness, authority and luxury. Red conveys activity and energy. It's emotion, passion and love. On the downside, red can sometimes be perceived as aggressive. Think about Red Bull. Blue is a colour used by established companies such as IBM. It conveys trust, sometimes comfort, reliability and also faith. Ford and Samsung use blue extensively in their branding. Green conveys calmness, relaxation and hope for the future. Companies like Starbucks use a lot of green in their branding.

Step 3: Position your brand

There are three main ways you can position your brand.

1. Positioning on **price**.
2. Positioning in terms of your **customers**, in other words the people who are going to pay you.
3. Positioning around **service**.

If you are going to position yourself in regard to price, the three ways to do that are to price at the premium (high level), at the low end or at the midlevel.

For example, when it comes to cars Bentley is at the high end and Toyota vehicles are priced at the low end and mid-range.

If you going to position yourself based on customers, think about whom they are. Notice how Apple tends to attract creatives such as people involved in the media and design industries. If you are going to position yourself based on service think about what that will mean specifically – for example, will it be speed, guarantees or convenience?

Step 4: Deliver your brand promise

Building a great brand is about building trust. How do you build trust and create loyalty to your brand? It all comes down to this – creating relationships with customers by setting very high **standards.**

Take Zappos as an example. It is one of the biggest online retailers of shoes in the world and part of their brand promise is that no matter when you buy shoes from them, you can return them for a full refund no matter when you bought them. That policy has created so much trust within their customer base that they will keep on buying.

It takes a long time to build trust, but that trust can be broken in a matter of seconds.

Do you have any questions or pressing
challenges at the moment?
Book your FREE 30 Minute
Business Success Session
(value of $497) now at
www.faceitandfixitbook.com

"A brand for a company is like
a reputation for a person. You
earn reputation by trying to
do hard things well."

Jeff Bezos, Founder, Chairman & CEO of Amazon

5. How to Fix Sales Problems

As my friend Blair Singer often says, Sales = Income.
So it therefore follows that:
No Sales = No Income.

It is always possible to boost sales. Often sales opportunities are right under your nose.

One of my mentoring clients was the owner of a hairdressing salon. Together we developed an approach to selling that increased their turnover by 50%. The idea was very simple and, with hindsight, so obvious. It goes without saying that chatting is very much part of the experience of going to have your hair cut. The idea that we came up with was to control and to direct the conversations that were taking place between the hairstylists and the clients. The hairstylists would subtly direct the conversation onto the problems the client might be having with their hair. And from knowing in some detail about the problems they were having, the stylists were able to sell the benefits of the various haircare products that the salon offered.

I worked with a doctor in Germany who was becoming frustrated with the fact that all she seemed to be doing was seeing patients and issuing them with prescriptions for drugs. She had an interest in the fields of health and nutrition. The idea that we put in place was for the doctor to buck the trend and to offer a range of complimentary health and nutrition products that she had a passion for.

Selling is easy when you know how. Here is a 6-step sales process that I have used in my businesses and with my clients to massively improve sales.

Step 1 – Figure out precisely who you are selling to

The first step in the process of bringing in sales is to identify your ideal client. This is important because there is a common misconception that, just because you have a great product or service, everybody will want to buy it.

There are millions of people out there that could be your customers. But not all of them are the right fit for your business. So you need to come up with a profile of your ideal client and then go out to target them.

To identify your ideal client the first step is to consider demographics and psychographics by answering the following questions.

- Are they male or female or both?
- What is their age range?
- What is their ethnicity?
- Where do they live?
- What do they do for a living?
- What is their level of income?
- What is their marital status?
- Do they have children?
- What are their interests?
- What are their politics?
- What things in life do they value?
- What are their aspirations in life?

If you are targeting businesses – are your ideal clients start-up companies, small and medium-sized enterprises or big corporations?

The second step is to go deeper and build a detailed picture in your mind of your ideal clients. Give them a name and describe what they are like. For example, you could say something like this

– John is 34 years old, he is married with two children, he lives in the southeast of England, earns £50,000 a year, likes rugby, watches CNN and reads the *Daily Telegraph.*

What this information allows you to do is to know what marketing messages to use. Knowing exactly what your ideal client is like means that you are more able to come up with messages which will resonate with them. The work you put into identifying your ideal client will save you a lot of money and a lot of time in the future.

Step 2 – Find and approach your ideal clients

The next step is to approach and contact your ideal clients. There are various methods you can use to do this and here are a few examples.

Cold calling is making unsolicited visits or telephone calls to a prospect when they are not expecting your call and know nothing about you. This approach is not for everyone but can work really well.

Networking is where you meet potential prospects face-to-face at meetings and gatherings. Some organised networking events occur regularly and others are more occasional.

Networking can work really well as long as you approach it in the right way.

Find networking events in your area and run some checks on them. How frequently are they on?

What type of people attend?

When you have done your research, pick two or three events to go along to. While there, decide if you think they could work for you. The idea being that you attend these events over a long period of time in order to build relationships.

When the other members of the networking organisation get to know and like you, they will come to trust you and will find it easier to make referrals to you. Some networking associations are very good at this. So you might want to visit several clubs to see which ones suit you.

When you attend networking events have your ears working well and do less talking. Listen to what people are saying. Get to understand what they're saying and see how you can help them first. You want to come across as being helpful to them. In turn, they will then want to reciprocate and help you. Networking is very powerful.

The old saying 'your net worth is in your network' is so true. My network has helped me a lot in the past.

As effective as it can be as a way of approaching prospects, I find that some people use **email marketing** as a bit of a cop out. What I mean by that is that sometimes people would rather run an email marketing campaign than get out from behind their computer and talk to people. Depending on the nature of your business, email may or may not be the answer. For example, if you do large deals you are not going to get any business done over email. For smaller value transactions, email can work well.

Have an open mind when it comes to social media. If it's all new to you and you don't want to go through the learning curve, get someone on your team who can support you with this. It is also possible to outsource social media marketing. Think of your social media pages as outposts. Use them to attract people to your business. You want them to call or email you so that you can then close them.

Referrals are a method very much linked with networking. But it can be a standalone method as well. For example, let's say part of your sales process is meeting new clients and speaking to them face-to-face. Before the end of the appointment you could ask this question: "Who else do you know who might be interested in this service?"

Step 3 – Build rapport

When you have found your ideal clients, what next? You need to establish positive relationships with them. When trying to establish an affinity with someone, the first thing you need to do is to "get into their world". Get to understand their challenges, their problems and some of the issues that they are facing within their business or their life.

Be interested in what they are saying. Ask questions. Too often sales people just want to talk, talk and talk. Instead of being interesting, be interested in them.

The next step is to verify what they are saying to you. Verifying shows that you have understood what they've said. It shows that you are not just paying lip service to what they're saying. By verifying, what starts to happen is you begin to get a shared reality.

Step 4 – Introduce and present yourself effectively

So you've defined your ideal client, you've met them and you have found out about them. So what happens when they ask you what you do? This is your moment. This is your time to present what you do in a very systematic and effective way.

I am going to show you a formula for developing a compelling way to present your information and to present yourself so that you grab the attention of the person you are talking to.

Before you actually start talking to someone you should be clear on what you want that person to do as soon as you have finished presenting. Do you want them to buy right now? Or do you want them to make an appointment with you? You might want them to ask you to put together a proposal. Because without being very clear on what you want, your buyer is not going to know how to react.

The Elevator Pitch Formula

Credibility is saying things that are true and which engage your prospect and make them want to learn more.

Here is an example. Let's say you are an accountant. You could simply say: "I am an accountant." But that statement doesn't build any credibility. When asked what you do what you say instead could be something along these lines: "For the last four years I have been working with hundreds of small business owners and helping them to decrease their costs and improve their bottom line by at least 15%. Is that something of interest to you?"

The difference between the two statements is credibility. In the second statement you have said how long you have been doing your job for and you have included some specific numbers in terms of the value you have added to your clients. Numbers and time give credibility.

What else gives credibility? Results do. Let's say you are involved in network marketing. How about when you introduce yourself to someone you say something like this: "I am part of an international team that, in the last 20 years, has helped thousands of people become financially free by being able to offer and distribute an exciting range of products and services." In this statement you have borrowed credibility from the network marketing organisation you are part of.

The most important part of this formula is the closing question. If you don't attempt to close, what you have just said just sits out there. Examples of closing questions include: "So is that something you would be interested in?" with "Can I show you how you can get involved? and "Is this something you are looking for?"

The key thing is to practice your elevator pitch. Drill it so that you get comfortable with it.

Step 5 – Handle objections

Have you ever been hit with an objection that you weren't able to deal with but 10 minutes later you came up with the perfect answer? Why is that? It's because when your emotions are high, your intelligence goes down.

High emotions = low intelligence.

So the key to handling objections is really knowing how to handle the emotions related to the objections.

There are only three main objections you are going to be hit with. The first is price, the second is time and third is lack of interest in what is being offered.

The first thing to do when you are hit with an objection is to acknowledge it by saying something like "Thank you" or "I understand". This is so that the person can see that you have heard what they have said. Most people want the acknowledgement to be there. You are not acknowledging that what they are saying is correct. All you are doing is acknowledging the fact that you have heard them.

The next thing to do is to ask a question. So say something such as: "Why do you say that?" or "Why is it too expensive?" In doing this, you are getting the prospect to start thinking and to start selling themselves.

It is not the person who talks the most that sells the most. It is the person who asks questions the most. Because whoever is asking the questions, is the one that is in control of the conversation.

Why ask questions? It's because you want to get down to the truth. You want them to tell you the real reason for saying what they have said. Because most of the time when people give you an objection, the first objection is not actually the real one. It's just a disguise or an habitual answer. People get so many sales calls that they often just get into the habit of saying that they are not interested.

When you find the truth, then you need to pivot the conversation back into your favour and move towards concluding a deal.

Step 6 – Close the deal

Your aim is to close deals authentically and ethically. Make sure your client is going to get exactly what they want. Some people think that sales is all about techniques. Techniques are important, but it's much more about your attitude and your intention to close the deal.

At a subconscious level, a prospect is looking for three things from you as the salesperson. They are clarity, confidence and conviction.

- Am I clear on exactly what I am being asked to buy here?

- Do I have faith in this person? Do I have confidence that they can actually deliver what they are promising?

- Do they know what they're talking about? Can they really deliver?

Closing techniques

There are hundreds of closing techniques and here are a couple.

The **Silent Close** is where you make your final closing statement and then go silent immediately afterwards. If an uncomfortable silence follows, remain silent. The theory here is that whoever speaks first will lose.

The **Assumptive Close** is where you summarise what you have said and then end by assuming the sale and, for example, asking the prospect how they'd like to pay. So you never actually ask the prospect if they want to buy. It is then down to the prospect to protest that they have not indicated that they are interested in buying.

Step 7 – Follow up

After a period of time, go back to your new clients and find out how they're getting on. If they're not happy, then you can correct the problem. If they are happy, then you can ask for a testimonial.

Step 8 – Get powerful testimonials

The ideal structure for a testimonial from a customer is what is known as a 'before and after'. This means that the customer says how things were before they started using your product or service and ends by saying how things are now.

It is a good idea to write a testimonial for your customer based on what they tell you in terms of the results they received. Then send it to them for their approval.

> **Do you have any questions or pressing challenges at the moment? Book your FREE 30 Minute Business Success Session (value of $497) now at www.faceitandfixitbook.com**

"The top salesperson in the organization probably missed more sales than 90% of the sales people on the team, but they also made more calls than the others made."

Zig Ziglar

6. How to Fix Financial Problems

Generally speaking businesses get into financial difficulties because they avoid thinking about it as much as they need to, fail to manage cash flow, get their pricing wrong and don't get the right kind of professional help.

I had a financial services recruitment company in London as a client a few years back. They opened up for business located in a very expensive office block near Liverpool Street in the City. They had huge expectations of early success. But cash didn't come into the business as quickly as they thought it would do. We talked it through and, despite the cash flow issues, they remained reluctant to give up their expensive premises. But I was very clear with them that they needed to face up to the facts. In the end they decided to downsize and move to new premises in Essex. Their premises costs were a quarter of what they were paying in central London, which improved their cash flow. They have since gone from strength to strength.

In the early days of running a business it is crucially important to identify how much money your business will require. This not only includes the costs of starting, but the costs of staying in business. It is vital to take into consideration the fact that many businesses take a year or two to get going. This means you will need enough funds to cover all costs until sales can eventually pay for these costs.

If you have started a company and it is struggling with very little capital, you're not in a very good position to go to the bank to ask for another loan.

Be realistic at the beginning and start with enough money that will last you to the point where your business is up and running and cash is actually coming in. Trying to stretch your finances at the beginning may mean that your business never gets off the ground, and you'll still have a lot of cash to repay.

If you don't have enough cash to carry you through the first six months or so before the business starts making money, your prospects for success are not good. What you should do is to consider both the business and your personal living expenses when determining how much cash you will need.

Managing money

You must understand and get a grip on the financial aspects of your business. Most business owners don't. This means that their finances do not get managed.

Too often business owners become scared of looking at the numbers. Do you love Excel spreadsheets? Some people do, some people don't. I used to be one of the many that don't. And that's the reason why I got into financial problems.

You have to do what you have to do as a business owner. Sometimes business owners get confused. They don't understand what they're looking at when it comes to the numbers. Some fall into a state of denial. They kid themselves that everything is okay and that there are no issues. And so often what they end up doing is managing their business from their bank balance and not from their financial statements.

They look at how much they have in the bank that day and use that figure as the basis for deciding what they can afford to spend.

What I'm saying here is that you need to take full responsibility for your financials. Start managing your money fully.

There is no old saying – cash is king. Cash is definitely king. Without cash, you can't operate your business fully. The key is to manage your cash using three important financial statements:

- The Profit and Loss Statement (sometimes called the income and expenses statement)
- The Balance Sheet
- The Cash Flow Statement

If you use your cash flow statement on an ongoing basis you will know how much cash is coming in, what is due in at a certain date in the future and what is due to go out. When you are familiar with that information, then you can plan.

You must manage your accounts payable and accounts receivable in an optimal way. Your aim should be to negotiate so that your clients pay you earlier and you pay your suppliers later. You should negotiate your contracts well so that you get the best deal possible.

This is about discipline. Its good business practice to make sure that you chase money you are owed when payment is due and you are also paying your suppliers when they are due payment.

You must always make sure you have your finger on the pulse of your business. Most business owners don't know what their business is doing on a day-to-day or week-to-week basis either operationally or financially.

Make it a practice to look through how your business is doing from the numbers point of view every week on a set day and time. Make a point of always knowing exactly what is going on in your business. Ask your bookkeeper or accountant to supply you with these reports every week – your cash flow report, your accounts receivables and your accounts payable.

Getting your pricing right

Deciding what to charge is not easy. Because there is so much competition, it can be difficult figuring out how to set your prices. But make sure that you don't set your prices arbitrarily. Some business owners look at the prices their competition are charging and base their pricing solely on that. First things first, though – your first consideration should always be your costs. You must make sure you don't set prices which lead to you making a loss. Next, consider the value that your products or services add to your clients and price accordingly.

Hiring professionals

How do you choose a bookkeeper or an accountant? What you are looking for with a bookkeeper or an accountant is timely information. This is so that you can make informed decisions about critical issues in your business at the right time. You are also looking for guidance and advice.

Tax advice is critical. You create wealth by improving profitability but you can also do so by understanding tax. When you know how the tax system works you can take advantage of it from a business point of view.

7. How to Fix Culture Problems

Culture – or context as I call it – is the internal environment in which a business operates. If you set up the context correctly your business can thrive under any economic circumstances.

Think of context as the container your business exists within. The context holds everything within the business – such as your marketing, your products, your policies and the services and your staff – together.

Imagine we had two identical businesses. One of the businesses is housed within a weak container and the other exists within a strong container. It's a bit like having a paper cup versus a ceramic cup. If you put pressure on the paper cup what happens? It starts to collapse. Eventually it will give in to the outside pressures. If you put pressure on the ceramic cup, however, it will stay stronger for longer.

The equivalent of a ceramic cup for a business is the existence of things such as a team where everyone understands the mission and where everyone abides by a set of rules that are all agreed upon. The context of the business is its environment and this includes things such as the mission, the rules and the goals.

Answering these questions will help you to create a better business context.

- What is it you do? Get very clear on that.
- Who do you do it for? Who are you really representing and working for in this world?
- What is the benefit that they get when they work with you?

Create your environment

This all comes down to knowing how to establish trust. What creates trust? Trust is created by **boundaries**. A boundary is something that confines a space. When people have boundaries it is easier for them to make decisions.

So, let's say for example you've promised to get back to a client within 24 hours. You have created a boundary. If you deliver within the boundary, that creates trust.

If you were to take a piece of silver out of a closed environment, it would start to discolour in an open environment where air could get to it. You would need to keep polishing it to make sure it stayed looking shiny and at its best.

Something similar happens with your people. We get conditioned over time to think and behave in certain ways. For example, we are often influenced by the media and the news coming from those outlets isn't always positive. Bad news sells, after all. What can happen over time is that your attitudes become negative and your energy gets sapped.

So to create a great business environment you've got to realize that deep down inside everyone is a very positive person just waiting to be let loose. The problem is that they have been conditioned to think and behave in a different way, which is not really the way they may actually want to think and behave.

Their mindset and their attitudes may be a bit rusty. So you have got to also know how to create a closed environment for your staff where the energy is amazing.

Create a Code of Honour

A Code of Honour is a set of rules that govern behaviours on a team. But this is not just any set of rules. This is a set of rules in relation to behaviours in a specific environment.

You typically get chaos when you have a team who don't know the rules. They just do what they want to do and they play by their own rules.

The great thing about a Code of Honour rather than an ordinary set of rules is that it is held together by everybody in the team.

This can be the difference between having a good team and having a great team.

A code of honour includes:

- supportive behaviours that are wanted; and
- non-supportive behaviours which are not wanted.

It is best to have no more than 12 rules/codes.

The idea is to make sure everybody is on the same page and has the same understanding of what the rules are.

When setting the rules it is important to get feedback. For example, different people might have different interpretations of what a particular rule means. So you need to check understanding and get agreement on each rule.

When someone breaks a rule it's very important that they get called on it. But it is important that the calling is done elegantly. You must do it in such a way that the self-esteem of the person who is being called is kept intact. This means, for example, speaking to them in private rather than in front of the rest of the team.

"Great players are determined by
their talent, desire and willingness
to play by the code."

Blair Singer

8. How to Fix Operational Problems

The absolute key is to set your business up so that it doesn't depend on you. As a business owner you need to transition from having a self-employed mentality to having a mindset of a true business owner. The way to do this is to systemise your business.

What is a system? It is set of processes. A process is a series of steps as to how to do something. The processes can't just sit in the head of the business owner. Otherwise the whole thing depends on one person. The processes need to be documented.

Systemising your business

This is all about getting things out of your head and the heads of your staff and onto paper. Here is one way of doing it.

- Walkthrough how you carry out a task with someone alongside you writing it all down. Say, for example, the task is welcoming a client. Role play the scenario. Use the words you would like your staff to say as the greeting. Move along each step of the process. Keep talking, sharing what you do at each stage and the best practices you use. Make sure it is all noted down. Alternatively you could perhaps use a Dictaphone as you carry out the task yourself.

- The next stage is to document your notes to turn them into step-by-step processes.

- Go through the process yourself. Follow it through to see if you have included everything and if the content is correct.

- Now trial it out. Get people from your team to follow the guidance notes. Some will do things better than others. So part of the trial is also about knowing how to train your staff to actually use the systems.

Documented processes make it much easier to recruit new people into your team and to train them. Did you know that it costs between 6 and 15 times more to attract new customers than it does to retain existing customers by building relationships with them?

Systemising Customer Service

You need to make sure you have forms for various situations and scripts for your team to use when handling particular customer issues and enquiries.

Bear in mind though that, while scripts are a good idea, it's also important that you teach your team how to be present with customers, how to listen to them and how to think on their feet in order to deal with nonstandard situations.

You must take customer service seriously. For example, consider getting an IT system for call handling that routes incoming calls to staff members who are free. If used properly, IT systems can help you to achieve more with less. Depending on the nature of your business, there are systems such as salesforce.com and Infusionsoft which can really help you to do that.

If you want to know how best to deliver customer service check out videos on YouTube about how Zappos approaches customer service.

Systemising Finance

Consider using systems such as Sage, QuickBooks, Xero and Kashflow.

Use professional business accounting software to keep records of all financial transactions, including every expenditure and all revenues received. Use this information to generate profit and loss statements. This is valuable information that you need to run your business, know where you stand at all times, and keep it operating in the black.

Systemising Marketing

There are only so many hours in a given day and time you waste as a business owner cannot be recovered. Plus there is only one of you.

That's why you should consider automating your marketing. There are tools available for automating your email and your social media campaigns. Examples include Infusionsoft for email marketing and

Hootsuite for social media marketing. Using Infusionsoft you can automatically follow up with your sales leads and schedule email broadcasts up in advance. Hootsuite enables you to do the same thing with regard to your social media posts.

Systemising Sales

Script out exactly what you want your sales staff to say. Not that they are going to say word for word what you include but, with a script, they will have an idea of the essence of what you want said.

The key here is to test and measure. Either set up an Excel spreadsheet or use a system such as salesforce.com to track the progress and the success rates of your sales efforts.

9. How to Fix Staffing Problems

Recruit effectively

As your business grows at some point you are going to need a team of people to work for you. Early on you may outsource some elements of your business, but sooner or later, especially if you have really grown, you will need a way of recruiting people into your team. The single best thing you can do when it comes to recruitment is to hire people based on their attitude. Look for a positive demeanour, the use of positive language, the way they speak and the way they project themselves.

You don't want to hire people who continually moan and seem to find wrong in everything. So hire on great attitude because otherwise that negativity will infect your business. The message is to hire on attitude and train the skill.

Also, it is important to take your time to recruit the right person. This way of doing it is going to be more cost effective for you than rushing the recruitment process, hiring the wrong person and then dealing with the hassles associated with hiring the wrong person. So hire slowly and fire quickly instead of the other way round.

The ideal situation is where people find you and want to work for you. This is because they come with the right attitude, are more loyal – plus it's cheaper because you don't incur the recruitment costs.

One of the best ways to recruit is to ask. Ask your friends, family, your business associates and your database of contacts. The advantage is that they will know what you are looking for. The other way is to use a job board or a recruitment agency.

Consider doing assessments such as psychometric testing. You need to know what your candidates are really like. You are not always going to get that at an interview so consider going out for lunch or for coffee to see how they behave in that environment.

If the laws of your country permit you to do so, consider giving your new hires a trial period to see how they behave in that environment.

Train effectively

Training is so important. It should be a regular thing so that staff can grow and do their job in a much better way.

A complaint that you often hear from business owners is that they're so busy that they don't have adequate time for staff training. One answer is to outsource the training.

My suggestion is that a training session is delivered at least once a quarter, if not once a month. You need to have that constant training routine in place so that staff know that they can build on their skills.

How you carry out training is important as well. The word education comes from the Latin word 'educe', which means to draw out. So training is not just about passing information and skills on to your staff. The brain doesn't retain information that well when training simply involves reading and passively listening.

10. How to Fix Customer Relationship Problems

Your customers may *like* your product or service but they perhaps might love it if you changed one feature or altered one of your processes.

- So when it comes to your customers, what are they telling you? Are you even listening?

- And when it comes to your marketplace, is it declining? Is there still a demand for what you're offering?

These are important questions to ask and to get answers to. You need to find out before it's too late.

A successful business keeps its eye on the trending values and interests of its existing and potential customers. Survey customers and find out what their interests are and keep abreast of changes and trends using customer relationship management (CRM) tools. Effective use of CRM can help keep your business from failing.

11. How to Fix Growth Problems

Business growth and expansion take as much careful and strategic planning as managing day-to-day operations. The key to successful growth and expansion is strategic planning and sound financial management.

Overexpansion often happens when a business owner confuses success with how fast they can expand their business. There is a lot to be said for controlled growth. Slow and steady wins every time. Dependable, predictable growth is vastly superior to spurts and jumps in volume. Many companies who rapidly expand end up bankrupt.

Going after all the business you can get drains your cash and actually reduces overall profitability. You may incur significant upfront costs to finance large inventories to meet new customer demand. Don't borrow so much that if the economy stumbles, you'll be unable to pay back your loans.

Don't repress growth, though, once you have an established solid customer base and a good cash flow. Let your level of success guide you in setting the right pace. Signs that you should consider expanding are:

- being unable to fulfil customer needs in a timely way; and
- employees having difficulty keeping up with production demands.

If you've done your research and analysis and expansion is warranted then you should treat the expansion like you're starting all over again. You should identify the systems and the people you will need to add in order for your business to grow. Then you can focus on the growth of your business without you doing everything in it yourself. If you don't do this, the financial drain of the failing side of the business can sink the whole company.

- If you're expanding the reach of your business, make sure that you understand the areas and markets into which you'll now be targeting.

- If you're expanding the scope and focus of your business, make sure you understand your new products, service and intended consumer as much as you do with your current successful business.

Successful and famous-name companies such as McDonalds carry out careful and thorough research and planning before opening a new restaurant location. Before they do anything they look at demographic data and trends and other relevant information such as future development plans for the area.

You must do the same for your business to avoid failure. Here are some tips:

- Conduct thorough research to ensure the time is right and the funding is available for expansion.

- Make sure the initial business is stable before expanding to an additional location.

- Don't order inventory you're not sure you can sell but have a plan already in place to fill orders quickly should the demand present itself.

"Try not to become
a man of success.
Rather become
a man of value."

Albert Einstein

Start Turning Your Business Around Now

If your business is struggling, you now have no excuses because:

- you now know the perils of not facing up to your problems;

- you know what the problems are that can bring down a business;

- you've been inspired by amazing business turnaround stories; and

- you've learned about a formula that you can use to turn around the fortunes of your business.

So get to it right away. Don't procrastinate any further. Depending on the state of your business, you may not have long to save it. So you must act now.

If you'd like any assistance, then feel free to get in touch. I am a Business Coach & Consultant and myself and my team are ready and willing to help you if you'd like help. You can contact me via my website –

Do you have any questions or pressing challenges at the moment? Book your FREE 30 Minute Business Success Session (value of $497) now at www.faceitandfixitbook.com

Resources

Books

The Power of Masterminding
by Mac Attram

Would you like to discover how to apply the secret that great achievers such as Thomas Edison, Charles Wrigley and Bill Gates used to accomplish their success?

The key reasons that people do not achieve their goals are because they don't stay focused on what they want and fail to collaborate effectively.

You can't achieve major goals all on your own. You need to use the minds and resources of other people. The idea of self-made millionaires is a myth. Every great achiever, whether knowingly or not, has used an approach called Masterminding® to get results..

Masterminding® is an advanced form of thinking and teamwork. It's about plugging your brain into the minds of others and benefiting from their ideas, experience and abilities. It's about a group of people working in harmony with each other to achieve individual or group objectives.

In this book you will learn:

- how to form and run your very own success team
- the Masterminding® mindset, skillset and process
- how to accomplish your goals quickly and without stress or struggle

- how to draw on your Masterminding® team for a continual flow of ground-breaking ideas, energy, inspiration, feedback, contacts and resources, confidence, encouragement, challenge and accountability

Masterminding® will revolutionise the way you work with other people and achieve results.

The Inspired Warrior's Code
by Mac Attram

This is not another self-help book that makes 'quick fix' promises.

You will learn:

- a powerful set of success principles and techniques

- a proven, rich and powerful approach to living that will bring you all that you desire in life and more

Mac Attram is a former national martial arts champion. For him martial arts is not a sport but a 'way of living' aimed at achieving self-perfection through the union of mind, body and spirit..

As with martial arts, you will only understand The Inspired Warrior's Code when you practice it. But when you do you will:

- have the ability to create miracles in your life

- possess the courageous mindset of a champion

- be able to enjoy intense and absorbing relationships with all the people in your life.

Services

Visit **www.MindSpaceBusiness.com** for more information

Training Events

Mac Attram runs an exclusive selection of live training workshops, boot camps and webinars in the arena of wealth creation, business development and personal success for entrepreneurs and business owners each year.

All of Mac's live events are intensive, interactive and highly-experiential, designed to bring you lasting improvement...

- Grow your sales rapidly using our proprietary method.
- Discover the secrets to success in life, business and money- from the leading business and personal growth expert.
- Gain clarity on the steps you must take to achieve your goals.
- Learn how to deal more effectively with negative & self-limiting thoughts, so that fear, doubt, confusion or frustration no longer hold you back.
- Understand what shifts you need to make in your thinking – and how to actually make those shifts.
- Reprogram your mind to become more "success conscious" through exclusive solo, partner and group exercises – and make greater success your natural path.
- And much more... including meeting and networking with likeminded people.

Mentoring

Our 1-on-1 mentoring for entrepreneurs and business owners is designed to:

- Help you decide what goals and dreams are most important to you, so that you become laser-focused on the important things.

- Create a strategic plan to help you achieve those goals.

- Establish a realistic action plan so that you meet all important milestones.

- Implement an effective dashboard to track & measure all your key performance numbers, so that you know how you are doing at any given time of the month or year.

- Discover the "subconscious thoughts" that are holding you back, and then help you blast through them to achieve the life you want and deserve.

- All of these and much more will help you stay accountable, take action, solve business problems, and ultimately, progress faster and achieve higher levels of success than you'd achieve on your own.

Incubating

This is our ultimate partnering solution for supporting business owners who have an early stage business with high growth potential, who want to accelerate the growth and profitability of their business in both the short and the long term.

New business ideas are fragile and the chances of success can be increased with nurturing. With Incubating, we take an equity stake in your business and provide consistent, ongoing, 1-on-1 support to help nurture you and your business to grow stronger and faster.

Areas we can support you with include:

- Sales Performance
- Marketing
- Team Building & Training
- Strategic Planning
- Operational Profits
- Financial Performance
- Legal Context
- Customer Service
- Systems & Processes

Our goal is to help you build a business that can be run as a cashflow-generating asset that works with or without you – and which can later be sold or prepared for IPO.

Speaking

Mac is a world-class keynote speaker who engages, inspires and empowers audiences. He has masterfully spoken at and facilitated large seminars, conferences, exhibitions and corporate functions.

Masterminding

Masterminding is when a group of people come together in a spirit of cooperation and harmony to achieve goals, be they shared ones or individual ambitions.

The key idea is to coordinate the combined knowledge, creativity and effort contained within the group in order to achieve common and individual objectives.

There is nothing new about Masterminding. Whether utilized knowingly or not, almost all of the great accomplishments of history were achieved using this method.

Mac Attram is the author of the book, The Power of Masterminding, and is one of world's leading facilitators of the masterminding process.

A couple of times a year, he leads exclusive and invitation-only Masterminding events at beautiful locations around the world.

About the Author

Mac Attram is a multi-award winning speaker, investor, mentor, incubator, educator and author. In the world of business he is best known for helping entrepreneurs grow their businesses rapidly and for performing business turnarounds. He has trained and coached tens of thousands of business owners and individuals in over 15 countries around the world. He has shared the stage with some of the world's premier thought leaders and speakers, including Robert Kiyosaki, T. Harv Eker, Blair Singer, Bill Walsh, Keith Cunningham, James Caan, Duncan Bannatyne and Les Brown.

Printed in Great Britain
by Amazon

85114873R00071